D1288697

Pebble®
Bilingüe/
Bilingual

En el espacio/Out in Space

Los planetas/The Planets

por/by Martha E. H. Rustad

Editora consultora/Consulting Editor: Gail Saunders-Smith, PhD

Consultor/Consultant: Roger D. Launius, PhD
Curador principal/Senior Curator:
División de Historia Espacial/Division of Space History
Museo Nacional del Aire y del Espacio/National Air and Space Museum
Smithsonian Institution, Washington, D.C.

CAPSTONE PRESS
a capstone imprint

Pebble Books are published by Capstone Press,
151 Good Counsel Drive, P.O. Box 669, Mankato, Minnesota 56002.
www.capstonepub.com

Printed in the United States of America in North Mankato, Minnesota.
032010
005740CGF10

Books published by Capstone Press are manufactured with
paper containing at least 10 percent post-consumer waste.

Library of Congress Cataloging-in-Publication Data
Rustad, Martha E. H. (Martha Elizabeth Hillman), 1975–
     [Planets. Spanish & English]
     Los planetas = The planets / por Martha E.H. Rustad.
     p. cm.—(Pebble bilingüe. En el espacio = Pebble bilingual. Out in space)
     Summary: "Photographs and simple text introduce the planets in our solar
system—in both English and Spanish"—Provided by publisher.
     Includes index.
     ISBN 978-1-4296-5341-1 (library binding)
     1. Planets—Juvenile literature. I. Title. II. Title: Planets. III. Series.
QB602.R8618 2011
523.4—dc22   2010005000

Note to Parents and Teachers

The En el espacio/Out in Space set provides the most up-to-date
solar system information to support national science standards.
This book describes and illustrates the planets in both English and
Spanish. The photographs support early readers in understanding
the text. This book also introduces early readers to subject-specific
vocabulary words, which are defined in the Glossary section. Early
readers may need assistance to read some words and to use the
Table of Contents, Glossary, Internet Sites, and Index sections of
the book.

Table of Contents

Earth 5

The Solar System 9

Distance from the Sun 17

Glossary 22

Internet Sites 22

Index 24

Tabla de contenidos

La Tierra 5

El sistema solar 9

La distancia desde el Sol . . . 17

Glosario 23

Sitios de Internet 23

Índice 24

Earth

Earth is the third
planet from the Sun.
You can see Earth's water
and land from space.

La Tierra

La Tierra es el tercer
planeta desde el Sol.
Puedes ver el agua y el suelo
de la Tierra desde el espacio.

Sun/
Sol

Earth/
Tierra

A planet is a large object
that moves around the Sun.
Earth moves around
the Sun once each year.

———————————

Un planeta es un objeto grande
que se mueve alrededor del Sol.
La Tierra se mueve alrededor
del Sol una vez cada año.

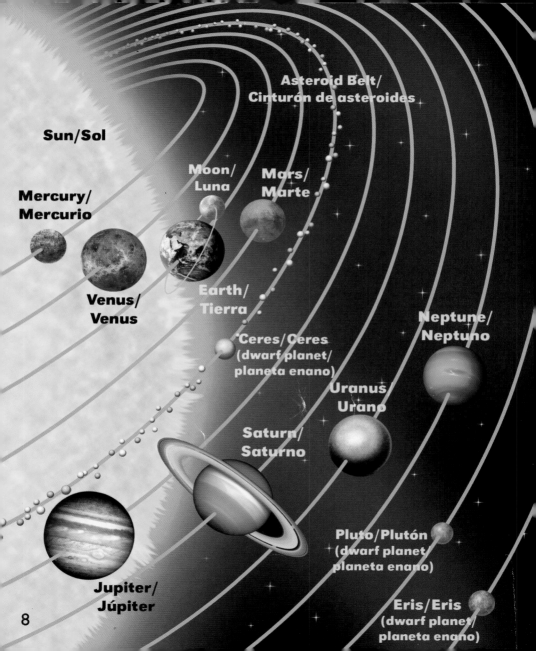

Sun/Sol

Mercury/
Mercurio

Venus/
Venus

Moon/
Luna

Mars/
Marte

Asteroid Belt/
Cinturón de asteroides

Earth/
Tierra

Ceres/Ceres
(dwarf planet/
planeta enano)

Neptune/
Neptuno

Uranus
Urano

Saturn/
Saturno

Jupiter/
Júpiter

Pluto/Plutón
(dwarf planet/
planeta enano)

Eris/Eris
(dwarf planet/
planeta enano)

8

The Solar System

Planets, dwarf planets, asteroids,
and comets move around the Sun.
These objects and the Sun
make up the solar system.

El sistema solar

Los planetas, los planetas enanos,
los asteroides y los cometas
se mueven alrededor del Sol.
Estos objetos y el Sol forman
el sistema solar.

Jupiter/Júpiter

Saturn/Saturno

Uranus/Urano

Neptune/Neptuno

Jupiter, Saturn, Uranus, and
Neptune are large planets.
They are made of gases.

Júpiter, Saturno, Urano y
Neptuno son planetas grandes.
Ellos están compuestos de gases.

Earth/Tierra

Mars/Marte

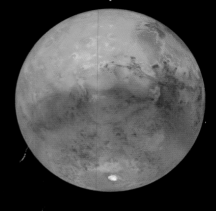

Mercury/Mercurio

Venus/Venus

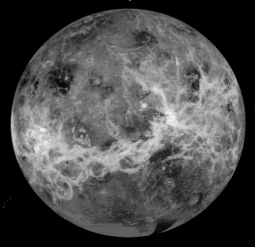

Earth, Mars, Mercury,
and Venus are smaller
planets. They are rocky.

———————————————

La Tierra, Marte, Mercurio
y Venus son planetas más
pequeños. Ellos son rocosos.

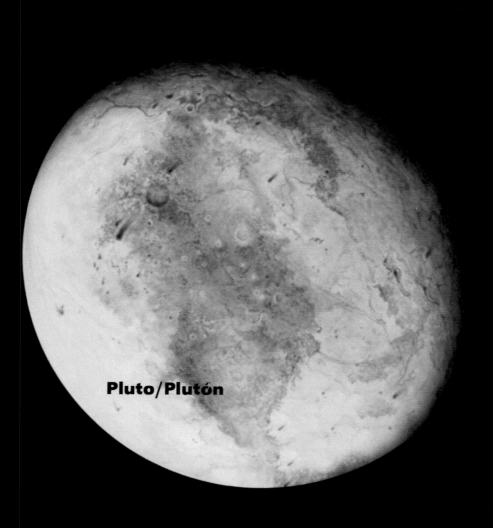

Pluto/Plutón

Pluto, Ceres, and Eris
are smaller than planets.
They are dwarf planets.
Dwarf planets are
made of rock and ice.

Plutón, Ceres y Eris son más
pequeños que los planetas.
Ellos son planetas enanos.
Los planetas enanos están
compuestos de roca y hielo.

Sun/Sol

Mercury/
Mercurio

Venus/
Venus

Surface of Venus/
Superficie de Venus

Distance from the Sun

Mercury and Venus
are close to the Sun.
These planets are very hot.

La distancia desde el Sol

Mercurio y Venus
están cerca del Sol.
Estos planetas son
muy calientes.

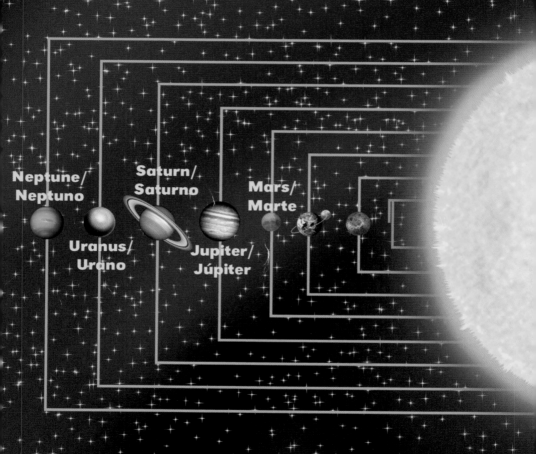

Neptune/
Neptuno

Uranus/
Urano

Saturn/
Saturno

Jupiter/
Júpiter

Mars/
Marte

Mars, Jupiter, Saturn,
Uranus, and Neptune
are far from the Sun.
These planets are very cold.

———————————

Marte, Júpiter, Saturno,
Urano y Neptuno están
lejos del Sol. Estos planetas
son muy fríos.

Earth's place near the Sun
gives Earth light and heat.
The Sun helps plants grow.
Earth is just the right
distance from the Sun.

———————————

La ubicación de la Tierra cerca
del Sol le da a la Tierra luz y
calor. El Sol ayuda a que las
plantas crezcan. La Tierra está a
la distancia perfecta del Sol.

Glossary

asteroid—a large rocky body that moves around the Sun

comet—a ball of rock and ice that moves around the Sun

dwarf planet—a round object that moves around the Sun but is too small to be a planet

gas—a substance that spreads to fill any space that holds it

solar system—the Sun and the objects that move around it; our solar system has eight planets, dwarf planets including Pluto, and many moons, asteroids, and comets

Sun—the star that the planets and dwarf planets move around

Internet Sites

FactHound offers a safe, fun way to find Internet sites related to this book. All of the sites on FactHound have been researched by our staff.

Here's all you do:

Visit *www.facthound.com*

Type in this code: 9781429653411

Glosario

el asteroide—un cuerpo rocoso grande que se mueve alrededor del Sol

el cometa—una bola de roca y hielo que se mueve alrededor del Sol

el gas—una sustancia que se extiende para llenar cualquier espacio que la contenga

el planeta enano—un objeto redondo que se mueve alrededor del Sol pero es muy pequeño para ser considerado un planeta

el sistema solar—el Sol y los objetos que se mueven a su alrededor; nuestro sistema solar tiene ocho planetas, planetas enanos incluyendo a Plutón, y varias lunas, asteroides y cometas

el Sol—la estrella alrededor de la cual giran los planetas y los planetas enanos

Sitios de Internet

FactHound brinda una forma segura y divertida de encontrar sitios de Internet relacionados con este libro. Todos los sitios en FactHound han sido investigados por nuestro personal.

Esto es todo lo que tienes que hacer:

Visita *www.facthound.com*

Ingresa este código: 9781429653411

Index

asteroids, 9

Ceres, 15

comets, 9

Earth, 5, 7, 13, 21

Eris, 15

Jupiter, 11, 19

Mars, 13, 19

Mercury, 13, 17

Neptune, 11, 19

Pluto, 15

Saturn, 11, 19

Sun, 5, 7, 9, 17, 19, 21

Uranus, 11, 19

Venus, 13, 17

Índice

asteroides, 9

Ceres, 15

cometas, 9

Eris, 15

Júpiter, 11, 19

Marte, 13, 19

Mercurio, 13, 17

Neptuno, 11, 19

Plutón, 15

Saturno, 11, 19

Sol, 5, 7, 9, 17, 19, 21

Tierra, 5, 7, 13, 21

Urano, 11, 19

Venus, 13, 17

Editorial Credits

Strictly Spanish, translation services; Katy Kudela, bilingual editor; Kim Brown, set designer and illustrator; Eric Manske, designer; Laura Manthe, production specialist

Photo Credits

Digital Vision, cover; NASA, 14; NASA/JPL, 1; NASA/JPL, 8 (Neptune and Venus); NASA/JPL, 10 (Neptune); NASA/JPL, 12 (Venus); NASA/JPL, 16 (both Venus images); NASA/JPL, 18 (Neptune and Venus); NASA/STScI, 8 (Jupiter and Saturn); NASA/STScI, 10 (Jupiter and Saturn); NASA/STScI, 18 (Jupiter and Saturn); NASA/USGS, 8 (Mars and Uranus); NASA/USGS, 10 (Uranus); NASA/USGS, 12 (Mars); NASA/USGS, 18 (Mars and Uranus); NASA/USGS/GOES, 4; NASA/Visible Earth, 8 (Earth); NASA/Visible Earth, 12 (Earth); NASA/Visible Earth, 18 (Earth); Photodisc, 8 (Mercury); Photodisc, 12 (Mercury); Photodisc, 16 (Mercury); Photodisc, 18 (Mercury); Shutterstock/Wojciech, 20

7116